TRANSFORMING GRACE

LESLIE MARTIN

Phoenix, Arizona

Transforming Grace

Published by New Mercies
12612 N Black Canyon Hwy.
Phoenix, Arizona, 85029 USA
www.calvaryphx.com
October, 2009
ISBN: 978-9825686-0-6

PRINTED IN THE UNITED STATES OF AMERICA

Transforming Grace

Contents

Transforming Grace

Dedication

Transforming Grace is enthusiastically dedicated to my husband, Mark. Honey, you were the first one to share God's amazing grace with me, and I am eternally grateful. You are the most grace oriented pastor/teacher I have ever heard and the best husband in the whole wide world! Thank you for loving, supporting and encouraging me in grace, in ministry and in writing this book. You are an amazing man of God, and I'm so proud of you.

Special Thanks

A book is never the product of just one person, and this book is no exception. I am so grateful to the following people:

To Mark, Emily, Ellie and Daniel – my incredible family. You were always there to inspire and encourage me during this process and never complained about taking charge of things I usually do to give me study, ministry and writing time. Thanks Mark for all your suggestions, coming up with the title and helping with the cover ideas. I see where our children get their artistic talent for visual arts! You are all gifts from God and the best family in the whole wide world!

Transforming Grace

To Karen, my wonderful personal assistant. You have spent countless hours transcribing, editing and working to put this book into print. Thanks for telling me that you were going to "lock up my manuscript" so I couldn't edit it yet another time... I don't know if it would have ever been printed! You are an amazingly gifted person, and I'm so blessed to serve Jesus with you, friend.

To Shawn. Thanks so much for lending your incredible artistic gift in creating the cover for *Transforming Grace*.

To Brenda, Cami and Therese. Wow, thanks, thanks, thanks for reading my manuscript and for your insightful suggestions, edits and encouragements.

To Mary, my infusion nurse. You were such a great cheerleader every time I came in for my intravenous infusion (carrying my manuscript). You showed such a genuine interest in the book I was trying to write. Can you believe it? It's finally done!

Introduction

Transforming Grace

One of the things that we can count on is that we will experience many changes throughout our lives. Our work changes and where we live may change. We experience change as we grow older and our children start their own families. You may be a young adult who can't wait to get out there and change the world. Perhaps, you have lived a few decades and you have seen many changes in your life – some for the good and some for the worse. Whoever we are and whatever we have encountered, we have all experienced change. By far, the best and most radical change that has happened to me was when God turned everything around and gave me a whole new life through His grace.

When God's grace first dawned on me, I was a young college student with no idea how much His grace would transform everything in my life. Grace made an initial, radical difference in my relationship with God. Before I understood God's grace, I had a spiritual ache, a longing to know that He loved me and that I could have assurance of salvation. Even though I was deeply religious and devout, my faith was dry and I felt a million miles away from God. I didn't have any hope that I would go to heaven someday. I was caught in a treadmill of trying to change for the good, but only finding myself making no progress. I was desperate for love, acceptance and assurance, but instead, I felt like a spiritual failure. The strict, legalistic church I had grown up in didn't have answers to my questions or assurances that I could know that I was saved. All that my teachers and pastors could say was, *Just do the best you can to keep the rules and be a good girl. Hopefully, you'll make it to heaven.*

But, one morning as I was reading my Bible, God's grace shone through the fog of religious legalism. I was completely astonished to read, *"And the testimony is this, that God has given us eternal life, and this life is in His Son. He who has the Son has the life; he who does not have the Son of God does not have the life. These things I have written to you who believe in the name of the Son of God, so that you may* **know** *that you have eternal life.*"[1]   A quiet thought came to me, *'Do you believe in Jesus?'* *'Of course I believe,'* I responded. *'Then you can* <u>know</u> *you are saved.'*   My church had told me I **couldn't** know; the best I could do was **hope** that I'd make it to heaven.   The fog of legalism and the lies of uncertainty evaporated!   In that moment I *knew* I was saved, even though my church had taught me that I couldn't know.   The Bible said that I **could** know, and that I was going to spend *eternity* with God!

---

[1] 1 John 5:11-13 (NASU) (Emphasis added by author)

Transforming Grace

What I didn't know at that time was how radical God's grace would be in transforming -- not only my future destination -- but everything in my life! Understanding God's grace eventually led my husband and me out of cultic legalism and gave us the strength and faith we needed to leave the church that our families had been a part of for four generations. We temporarily lost our relationships with family and friends during that time as they shunned us for leaving the *only true church* (their terminology), but since then, God's grace has worked its miracle in many of their lives as well and we have seen all our family and many from that cultic denomination transformed by grace. Understanding God's grace has challenged our thinking, our relationships to others and every part of our lives. Such a small word, *grace,* from such a big God was essential to my understanding God's love for me, so that I could love Him and others freely, with my whole heart. I had religious, moral training, but without grace, I didn't have the freedom to give or receive the love that would give me hope, peace and strength for every day.

God's amazing grace has changed, and still does change everything! As you continue to consider how grace transformed the lives of the woman at the well, the woman caught in adultery, and others mentioned in this book, ask yourself, *How has God's grace transformed my* *life?* My prayer is for you to be able to embrace this great big God, the God of *Grace.*

Transforming Grace

Chapter One

What is Grace?

When God's grace comes into a person's life, His grace transforms everything! That statement may seem too wide and deep a claim at first, but as we come to understand what grace is all about and experience God's grace for ourselves, we will find that His grace truly makes everything new in our lives. The men and women of the Bible who came to know God's grace were completely changed by it. We can see the incredible grace of God in transforming lives in people like Paul (a former persecutor of Christians), Peter (a man who denied

Transforming Grace

Jesus publicly), and Mary Magdalene (a woman involved in the occult who had been possessed by seven demons before Jesus set her free). These examples, and many others throughout the Bible, show us that God will love and accept anyone, no matter what they have done, if they will accept the gift of His loving grace.

You may not have a very good idea of what grace is all about. You may have heard Christians use the word – but it's unclear exactly what they mean. On the other hand, if you are a Christian, you are probably familiar with the term *grace.* You've heard pastors talk about grace, and you've sung dozens of hymns and worship songs thanking God for His grace. Yet, even Christians can have an incomplete or fuzzy understanding of God's grace. The Bible words translated as *grace* in the Old Testament Hebrew and the New Testament Greek are nearly the same:

> kindness, favor, extending of favor,
> <u>often when it is neither expected nor deserved</u>...[2]

Grace has elements of kindness and mercy, yet it is an even more astonishing expression of love. When a person receives mercy, he is not punished for his

[2] Vine's Expository Dictionary of Biblical Words, Copyright © 1985, Thomas Nelson Publishers. Biblesoft's New Exhaustive Strong's Numbers and Concordance with Expanded Greek-Hebrew Dictionary. Copyright © 1994, 2003, 2006. Biblesoft, Inc. and International Bible Translators, Inc.

wrongdoing. Mercy says, *I won't punish you.* Grace goes beyond mercy! Grace says, *I will take your punishment for you and pour undeserved blessings into your life.* Mercy doesn't give us the consequences we deserve, and grace gives us blessings that we don't deserve.

To really understand and appreciate God's transforming grace, we have to see it in contrast to the mess we have made in our lives. God's grace shines the brightest when we see our dark, hopeless condition apart from His grace. Most of us will honestly admit that we have said hurtful and hateful things we wish we could take back, and we have made selfish choices and hurt others in the process. We have lied, cheated and taken that which doesn't belong to us. We've been sexually immoral and addicted to pornography. We have hurt other people's reputations by hearing some dirt about them and without checking to see if it is really true, we have believed the worst and even passed along the lie to someone else. Some of us have been abusers, alcoholics, drug addicts or criminals. Still others of us have been religious or moral hypocrites. We may be tempted to close this book in disgust, because we don't want someone telling us that our lives are anything other than good and upstanding. Stay with me here, don't quit reading yet. Whether we care to admit it or not each of us has a terrible problem – we're what the Bible calls *sinners*. Even the best among us doesn't have a shred of hope without God's grace.   God says that sinners cannot be with Him; sinners will not go to heaven but will face eternal punishment apart from God.

> *For the wages of sin is death.*
> (Romans 6:23)

Every one of us has earned a paycheck from God because of our sin; the paycheck reads *death*.   We're in big trouble with God because we're sinners, but the good news is that God **loves** sinners!   God loves you, and He loves me.   He doesn't want anyone to suffer eternal punishment, and He has made a way for His love to prevail and for us to escape judgment and experience life forever with Him.

That way is called His **grace**!

In the Bible, we find that God explains grace very simply:

> ...so that in the coming ages He might show the immeasurable riches of His grace in kindness toward us in Christ Jesus. (Ephesians 2:7, ESV)

Grace in its most basic definition is "God's kindness towards us in Christ Jesus." It's not that God is just kind. He showed His kindness towards us by sending Jesus to take our punishment. Jesus took our wages, the wages of sin - *death*. Jesus died for us. God's heart is kindness. He sees our miserable predicament, and He has made His grace the way for us to escape eternal punishment for our sins. Christ Jesus took our punishment when He died on the cross for us. Sin's wage is judgment for what we've done – death, but Jesus took the judgment we deserve. You probably know that Christianity is symbolized by a cross. Why a cross? Because Jesus died for you and me on a cross; His death was in my place and your place. If we accept God's grace, His kindness towards us in Christ Jesus, we will not be punished, and we will be given life forever!

Transforming Grace

> *For the wages of sin is death,*
> *but the free gift of God is*
> *eternal life in Christ Jesus our*
> *Lord.* (Romans 6:22)

On the cross, Jesus' hands were pierced with nails. His hands had never done anything to be punished by piercing, but our hands have done harsh and hateful things. His feet were nailed to the cross. His feet had never taken Him anywhere He shouldn't go, but our feet have taken us the wrong direction.

> *All of us have strayed away*
> *like sheep. We have left God's*
> *paths to follow our own. Yet*
> *the LORD laid on him the*

guilt and sins of us all. (Isaiah 53:6)

When Jesus hung on the cross, His head was crowned with thorns, yet He had never thought an impure or evil thought. We, however, have had many shameful thoughts. He took the punishment for us. It would be enough to be pardoned from our guilt and escape the deadly consequences of our sin, but grace goes even farther. Jesus took our punishment which we deserve and offers us the gift of eternal life with him which we don't deserve. That's grace!

You know the generous grace of our Lord Jesus Christ. Though He was rich, yet for your sakes He became poor, so that by His poverty He could make you rich. (2 Corinthians 8:9)

Transforming Grace

Chapter Two

Grace Looks for Us

One of the things we like to do as a family is to go on driving day trips. My husband Mark, I and our three children will set off from our home in Phoenix, Arizona. Usually, we end up heading north into the Rim Country, the forests of Prescott, the Verde Valley, the breathtaking red rocks of Sedona or the majestic mountains of Flagstaff. Several years ago, we found ourselves bouncing along on a rutty dirt road in the Verde Valley. The air was crisp and clean after a short, late summer rain, and we were out looking for adventure. We spotted a particularly beautiful prickly pear cactus loaded with red fruit and decided to take a closer look. Mark pulled the van over as far as he could on the side of the road, and we all piled out, tongs and buckets in hand, to pick prickly pear fruit. A few minutes later, we climbed into the van and tried to move, but the ground was too soft. The van was stuck in the wet, sandy soil. With one man and three elementary-age children trying to push, I endeavored to maneuver the van. As you can imagine, we didn't get very far! An hour or so later, with several rocks strategically placed under the tires and many heartfelt prayers, our vehicle finally made it back on the road, and we were on our way to civilization.

Transforming Grace

There are times when we get stuck in life. We may not be mired in the mud, but we are stuck in some hopeless situation. All our efforts seem futile as we struggle to extricate ourselves from our problem. Whether we are aware of it at the time or not, God cares, and He is already working to help us.

> *When we were utterly helpless, Christ came at just the right time and died for us sinners.* (Romans 5:6)

Jesus cares when we are stuck: stuck in sin, stuck in a self-destructive lifestyle, or stuck in hopelessness. He has a plan, and He will come through at just the right moment. When we are stuck, God's grace moves Him to find us. Help comes in the most unexpected way.

The Bible tells of a desperate woman who lived 2,000 years ago, who found herself stuck in a painful, hopeless life. She couldn't extricate herself from her problem; she was far away from God and part of a rejected people group called the Samaritans.

The Samaritans were related to the Jewish people and traced their lineage through the tribes of Ephraim and Manasseh. After the ten northern tribes of Israel were led away into captivity by the Assyrians and subsequently the southern kingdom of Judah was exiled by the Babylonians, there were only a handful of Jewish people left in the land. Those who remained began to intermarry with the foreigners that had been brought in to settle the land of Israel. In time, the remaining Jews abandoned or reinterpreted the covenant God had made with them and fashioned a corrupted form of religion that adopted biblical *and* pagan elements from the various religions of the people who had been brought in to settle the land. When the exiled Jews returned from their Babylonian captivity, they were appalled by their brethren's polluted form of religion and intermarriage with the pagan peoples. The returning Jewish exiles refused to reunite or reconcile with their brethren. By the time of Jesus, a deep animosity was firmly established between the Jews and their relatives, who had become known as the Samaritans.

With this historical background in mind, let's pick up the story of the hopeless Samaritan woman.

> *Therefore when the Lord knew that the Pharisees had heard that Jesus was making and baptizing more disciples than John (although Jesus Himself was not baptizing, but His disciples were), He left Judea and went away again into Galilee. And He had to pass through Samaria.* (John 4:1-4)

Transforming Grace

The Bible says Jesus **had** to pass through Samaria. Jews **never** passed through Samaria; they avoided it at all cost! When they traveled between Galilee in the North and Judah in the South, they would take a long detour around Samaria. They went many miles out of their way because of their hatred and distain for the so-called "half-breed" race of the Samaritans. Jesus was doing something very unusual, because He had a reason to go through Samaria. This is the only mention in the Bible of Jesus having to travel *through* Samaria. He probably went *around* Samaria with His disciples on other occasions, but this time He had a specific purpose. His heart of grace was moved to seek and find a terribly lost and confused woman. He would not only deliver her from her hopeless situation, but He would bring hope to all the Samaritans through her transformed life!

> *And He had to pass through Samaria. So He came to a city of Samaria called Sychar, near the parcel of ground that Jacob gave to his son Joseph and Jacob's well was there. So Jesus, being wearied from His journey, was sitting thus by the well. It was about the sixth hour. There came a woman of Samaria to draw water.* (John 4:4-7a)

Transforming Grace

In just a few verses we are given a picture of Jesus that is meant to remind us of one of the Jewish patriarchs, Jacob, the man who had dug this well. Here are the main elements of this picture: Jesus is weary from a long journey, He is sitting at a well at high noon, He is waiting for someone to arrive and He is getting ready to ask for a drink. Two thousand years before Jesus met the Samaritan woman at Jacob's well, Jacob, weary from a long journey, sat at high noon by a well, waiting for someone to arrive. At that ancient well, Jacob met Rachael, the woman who would become his bride. Jacob and Rachael would become the ancestors of the Jews and the Samaritans. The similarity of Jesus' and the Patriarch Jacob's experiences at the

well was not a mere coincidence. God
had orchestrated these events, although
they were two thousand years apart, to
open the door of the Samaritan woman's
heart to her conversation with Jesus. She
knew the stories of her ancestors, and as
she approached the well Jacob had dug
and saw this tired, dusty traveler, it may
have reminded her of Jacob's meeting
Rachael for the first time.

The Samaritan woman went to the well
at noon to avoid being around other
people, but, instead of turning away
when she saw Jesus sitting by the well,
she walked up to draw water.

> *Jesus said to her, "Give Me a drink."*
> (John 4:7b)

Transforming Grace

"Give Me a drink." She must have caught her breath a little at this request. Wasn't that the same question another ancestor, Rebekah, was asked at a well by a weary traveler? The Patriarch Abraham had sent his servant to find a bride for his son, Isaac. After a long journey, the servant prayed and asked God to show him who he was to ask to be Isaac's bride. The woman who agreed to give him a drink, and offered to water his camels, would be God's choice of a bride for Isaac. As Rebekah approached the well, the servant asked, *Please let me drink a little water from your jar. (Genesis 24:17)* This story may have flashed through the mind of the Samaritan woman; it is certainly another point of similarity that

Transforming Grace

God was using to draw her to Jesus. God took the initiative to reach out to this desperate woman through Jesus meeting her at the well and asking for a drink. God is always the One who takes the initiative in our lives. We're not the ones who move God; God moves us!

If you have a burden to pray for someone, if you have a desire in your heart to serve in some way, or if there is something you see that needs to be done for the Kingdom of God, God has probably placed that idea and desire on your heart and mind. You're not the one moving God by what you are doing. God is the One who has placed that on your heart because He always takes the initiative.

Transforming Grace

While the Samaritan woman quietly
prepared to draw water from the well,
Jesus asked her for a drink. Look how
gently He came to her. He could have
broken the silence of that stifling midday
and announced, *Here I am, the promised
Messiah!* But He didn't; He chose not to
overwhelm her. He just looked up at her
and asked, *May I have a drink?* He made
Himself very vulnerable. Jesus had
made this long journey with the specific
purpose of bringing hope and new life to
a group of people lost in the darkness of
sin and spiritual deception. Jesus'
vulnerability and willingness to engage
the woman in conversation opened up
her heart.

Transforming Grace

For His disciples had gone
away into the city to buy food.
(John 4:8)

This isn't an incidental detail. John is highlighting the fact that Jesus was alone at Jacob's well. Jesus wanted to talk to this woman without all of His disciples there. Considering her background, she probably wouldn't have talked to the Lord with a group of men standing around and listening in on the conversation. Had she seen thirteen men hanging around Jacob's well, she probably would have turned around while thinking to herself, *I'll just forget about getting water today.* God uses that same love and care in dealing with us. Details are not coincidental; rather, they are specifically designed to show us the extent of God's love to us.

Sychar, the woman's village, had its own well. She didn't have to travel this far to go to Jacob's well in the middle of the day. She went out of her way to go to a different well, at a time when other people wouldn't be drawing water, because she didn't want to be around anyone. She was not a popular person in Sychar: the men used and abused her and the women would think nothing of spitting in her face for that is the way women like her were treated in that culture.

> *Therefore the Samaritan woman said to Him, "How is*

it that You, being a Jew, ask me for a drink since I am a Samaritan woman?" (For Jews have no dealings with Samaritans.) (John 4:9)

It was not socially acceptable for a man to speak to a woman. It just wasn't done! Men didn't talk to women in public. They didn't even talk to the women in their own family in public. Jesus ignored this social restriction and spoke to a Samaritan woman. This was radical! On top of it all, she was a *sinful* Samaritan woman. At this point in her encounter with Jesus however, she wasn't ready to share that part of her life with anyone, especially a Jewish man.

Transforming Grace

What a demonstration of God's grace towards all of us! Jesus went around the customs and the prejudices of His time because He has a heart of grace and compassion for all lost and hurting people, regardless of race, gender or reputation. This poor woman had a lot of strikes against her, yet Jesus was there. He intentionally traveled through Samaria and sat at Jacob's well to talk, because He wanted share the water of the Word of Life with her.

> *Jesus answered and said to her, "If you knew the gift of God, and who it is who says to you, 'Give Me a drink,' you would have asked Him, and*

> *He would have given you*
> *living water."* (John 4:10)

Jesus knew the deep longing of her heart for hope and love. In His caring way of addressing this Samaritan woman, Jesus tenderly encouraged her, *I know your heart. I know that if you really knew who I was and what I was offering, you would readily respond to Me.* Jesus knew her heart. Everyone else thought she was a brazen sinner without a concern for eternal realities. But Jesus knew that deep down inside her sin-clogged heart she was crying out for a relationship with God. She longed for the Messiah! She was thirsty, not physically like Jesus, but deep down in her soul, she was thirsty for God. As we read further in the Bible's account of her story, one of the first topics she brought up was, *We know that Messiah is going to come! Are You really Him? Really?* There was a desire in her heart, and Jesus knew she would open up if she actually realized He was the promised Messiah. Jesus also knew how careful He had to be in talking with this woman who had been scarred with the hurts of society and sin.

This is encouraging as we consider the people around us. We may have been discouraged at the apparent lack of interest shown by our friends or family to the things of God. We may have thought something like this: *I've prayed for them forever! They are no nearer to Jesus than they were when I started. In fact, they are farther away. There is no hope. I give up! Forget it! This person is a lost cause!* We can lose heart in praying for the lost, because we can only observe their outward appearance and don't see their heart. God sees the heart. What is on the outside is not necessarily a reflection of what is on the inside. Outwardly, the Samaritan woman was perceived as an immoral, sinful person. On the inside, however, she was crying out for God. She was probably the person most receptive to Jesus in that entire city. God would use this woman to bring the message of grace to her people. When they saw her transformation and heard her testimony, their lives were changed. God is still using the story of this woman as an encouragement for us.

Transforming Grace

As described in the book of Acts, one of the first areas that heard the good news of Jesus after Jerusalem was Samaria. Philip, the evangelist, visited Samaria and saw a huge evangelistic movement explode among those rejected people. In village after village, the Samaritans turned to Christ with the result that there were thousands who came to believe in Jesus, the Messiah. (Acts 8:4-5)   I believe that what happened here by the well had a lot to do with the work that the Church was later going to do in Samaria.   The first seeds of God's grace were planted by Jesus in the heart of this sinful woman.

Transforming Grace

God's grace towards us is a grace that seeks and finds lost, hopeless, rejected people. His grace is for anyone and everyone. He goes the distance in taking the initiative in reaching out to us. Think about the time that you were stuck and far away from God; do you remember the moment that Jesus found you in your desperate mess? Perhaps you are experiencing that moment right now. Jesus' grace is a grace that finds us in the mess we have made in our lives. Don't hesitate to invite Him into the hopeless areas of your life where many questions lie unanswered. He can handle it all!

Transforming Grace

The Son of Man came to find
lost people and save them.
(Luke 19:10)

Transforming Grace

Chapter Three

Grace Satisfies Our Spiritual Thirst

The Samaritan Woman knew she was a desperate person. She was a notorious sinner, and, though everyone else had judged and rejected her, in her heart she was crying out for help. She was helpless to extricate herself from her miserable situation. Jesus knew, however, that she was prepared to accept Him when she understood He was the long-awaited Messiah. *"Jesus answered and said to her, "If you knew the gift of God, and who it is who says to you, 'Give Me a drink,' you would have asked Him…"* (John 4:10).

Transforming Grace

Our wonderful Jesus sees our heart. People can only see the outside, and based on their limited observations, they often draw an incomplete conclusion. Only God knows the inner longings of the soul. God understood the heart of this sinful Samaritan woman. Jesus knew that if she only realized Who He was, she would say, *Give me a drink. I want salvation; I accept You as the Messiah!* He looked right through the outward behavior and saw the inner person.

The fourth chapter in the book of John contains one of the longest conversations of Jesus recorded in the Bible. I think it's highly significant that He spent so much time with this despised Samaritan woman. Jesus places enormous value on people. He came to save *that which was lost* - not that which thought it had no need for a Savior. He came to seek those who know they have a need - a tremendous, huge, *gaping* need - and are desperate for help.

In His conversation with the Samaritan woman, Jesus revealed His identity. Up until this point in Jesus' ministry, He had only given hints about who He was and His mission. It wasn't until He met this woman that He freely revealed His identity. This is highly significant. He didn't even reveal Himself to His family as completely as He did to this woman. Similarly, He hadn't told His disciples that He was God the Messiah; but He told the Samaritan woman.

Jesus had many opportunities to reveal His identity. One prime opportunity had been at a recent Passover in Jerusalem. There were multitudes of people in Jerusalem for the Biblical celebration of Passover. It was one of three major feasts that the Jewish men were commanded to attend every year. At Passover, they made a pilgrimage from their homes to go to the temple in Jerusalem. It has been estimated that upwards of 180,000 people filled

Jerusalem during the Passover celebration.[3]

> *Now when He (Jesus) was in Jerusalem at the Passover, during the feast, many believed in His name, beholding His signs which He was doing. But Jesus, on His part, **was not entrusting Himself to them**, for He knew all men, and because He did not need anyone to bear witness concerning man for He Himself knew what was in man.*

---

[3] Taken from *Jerusalem in the Time of Jesus*, by Joachim Jeremias, Fortress Press Philadelphia © 1969 by SCM Press, Ltd. 2nd printing 1977, pp 77-79.

Transforming Grace

(John 2:23-25, emphasis added by author).

Many of Jesus' followers were a part of the multitudes crowding Jerusalem. They had come to believe in Him because of the signs and miracles He had done. They followed Him, but He did not reveal who He was to this huge crowd of believers. He did not reveal that he was God in the flesh, the Messiah, the Holy One who had been prophesied from the very beginning of this world to the first people God created, Adam and Eve. He didn't declare His identity to His disciples or His family. He told the least likely person. He chose to reveal the incredible revelation that He was the *I AM*, God in the flesh, to this Samaritan woman.

God does things differently than we would imagine, doesn't He? If I were planning Jesus' announcement of His Messiahship, I would have done it at the Passover where there were thousands of His followers, but God doesn't do things that way. He chose a small, dusty, out-of-the-way village in Samaria, a place no Jew ever visited. At that little well He met a despairing woman. The way God views things and the way we view things are very different, because God knows the end from the beginning. He knew that, not only was this Samaritan woman seeking a Savior, but that an entire town was also ready to receive a

Savior. There was an outcast community of Samaritans who were desperate for salvation.

Jesus seeks out the people with the greatest need. When He was born, who were the first to hear about it? *The shepherds in the fields!* It wasn't made known to the priests or announced to the scribes; it wasn't proclaimed to the Pharisees or the Rabbis. The good news was given to some lonely shepherds sitting out in the fields guarding their sheep at night. We can never guess how God is going to act. That makes things really exciting, doesn't it? We can't figure God out, but when He acts, the impact is incredible.

Jesus shared with the woman that He was the One who gives *living water.* *"You would have asked Him, and He would have given you living water."* (John 4:10) God meets us where we are. She had come to the well to draw water. Jesus, the Master Evangelist, met her at the well, and in that context He stated, *"If you were to ask me, I would have given you living water."* *Living water* means "to live." This isn't just ordinary water, the familiar H$_2$O which we drink every day. Living water is actually life-giving. *Life-giving!* It's not just something that quenches thirst and hydrates your body, but something that <u>gives</u> life. The term 'living water' also means *'lively or quick'* (to have movement). The phrase, *living water,* is actually speaking of flowing water, but a well is not flowing water, is it? No. A well is just a collection of water. There may be a spring that bubbles into the well, but the well is not a stream. A well is not the source of flowing water.

There were not many streams in Samaria. At Jesus' time, and even today, Samaria was very dry and desolate. Wells or cisterns, not streams, are the main source of water. Jesus exclaimed, If *you'd asked me, I would have given you running, abundant, lively, quick, flowing water.* Now, I think that piqued her curiosity because she replied, **Where are you going to get that? There's none of that around here. Are you greater than our father Jacob?**

Transforming Grace

"Living Water" not only gives life, but it is also flowing, *running* water. That kind of water is always fresh. Water that sits gets stagnant and algae grows on its surface. Have you ever camped by a pond or small lake? Many times, there is a shallow, reedy area along one or both sides of the pond. Would you want to go there, stick in your cup and get a drink? No way! That water is unpalatable. It has microscopic organisms growing in it. If you put it under a microscope, it would be very … *interesting*. That's what happens when water sits. It's *living* - that's for sure - but it's not filled with the life that I'd want to drink. God doesn't give us stagnant, algae-filled water. God gives us living, running, pure, refreshing water. That's the kind of water Jesus was offering to the woman – the water that would completely satisfy her spiritual thirst.

One summer, our church's high school group went backpacking on Snow Mountain in Northern California. Near the top of the mountain are picturesque alpine valleys and natural springs. One of the springs gushed from under a large, flat boulder. We stuck our sierra cups into the sparkling stream; there is nothing more refreshing than drinking ice cold spring water from a tin cup. Your lips almost freeze on the edge of the cup and it is so invigorating when you're parched and tired from hiking a steep mountain trail. We alternated between drinking the water and pouring it down our sweaty faces... It was so refreshing!

That's the kind of life-giving water that Jesus gives us; He's not offering some stagnant pool overrun with slime. He gives a never-ceasing flow of life; something new and refreshing from Jesus. The water that He gives, gives us life... It causes us to *truly* live.

Spiritual dryness and thirst are problems that have been around a very long time. Several hundred years before Jesus' conversation with the Samaritan woman at the well, her ancestors, the people of the kingdom of Judah (the Israelites or Jews), found themselves spiritually desolate and desperate as they were facing the armies of Babylon. At that time, the prophet Jeremiah lamented the terrible condition of his people as he declared God's message, *"For My people have committed two evils: They have forsaken Me, the Fountain of living waters, to hew for themselves cisterns, broken cisterns that can hold no water..."* (Jeremiah 2:13). Israel had two problems: 1) They rejected God, and 2) they tried to make life work on their own. These are contemporary problems. People all around us are spiritually dry - even Christians are spiritually parched and thirsty. God has what we need for true life, but so many people are repeating Israel's mistakes by ignoring God. They are trying to catch a few little drops of something that will keep them spiritually alive. God says this is committing a double evil. This is the heart of sin: leaving the Source of all life and trying to do something on your own. What will be the result if we try to store up a little strength and a little hope all on our own? We will be spiritually dry and thirsty, because all we can build is a broken cistern that can't hold water. When we aren't connected to the Source, we will not experience true life. As God looks on this world and sums up our most basic problems, there are two sins: 1) people have left the true Source, and 2) people try to find their own way to cope or succeed in life, but it ends in death.

Transforming Grace

When will people understand and turn
to God? When will they realize that they
are desperately thirsty for something
they cannot draw from the wells of this
world? Only when they finally come to
the spiritual desperation that
characterized the Samaritan woman will
they realize the futility of their lives
apart from God. The woman wasn't
thirsty after she had one husband; she
didn't even realize her need after two or
three husbands. She had to have five
husbands, and then be living with
someone else before she was at the point
of acknowledging her desperate thirst
for a Savior and His supply of living
water. Maybe the Samaritan woman
realized she was thirsty after the first
husband, but it didn't send her to Jesus.

It sent her to another husband then another and another. She wasn't satisfied with earthly love, because she was actually seeking the love of her Father. She needed the love that only God can give.

Like the Samaritan woman, God allows us to come to the point of realizing our spiritual dryness. What happens then? *"The afflicted and needy are seeking water, but there is none."* (Isaiah 41:17a) God patiently lets us sit by our little cistern until we get good and thirsty, and we're ready. We must realize that all the broken cisterns, dry wells and stagnant pools we've been trying have only left us dry and disappointed. That's the point at which God has a divine appointment with us, and He meets with us like he did with the Samaritan woman.

> *The afflicted and needy are seeking water, but there is none, and their tongue is parched with thirst; I, the LORD, will answer them Myself, as the God of Israel I will not forsake them. I will open rivers on the bare heights, and springs in the midst of the valleys; I will make the wilderness a pool of water, and the dry land fountains of water.* (Isaiah 41:17-18).

Transforming Grace

Isn't this an awesome promise? Are you dry and thirsty? Maybe you're 'saved' but you've gone out and dug a little well, a little cistern. You realize, *Hey, there is no water here.* Possibly, you've been looking for the love that only Jesus has for you: in relationships, in accumulating things, or in frantically filling your empty life with entertainment or work. There are a million little wells that people dig, *but they don't satisfy*. There is no water for a spiritually dry person apart from the true and living God. The only place that you are going to find refreshment and life is at the Source - the *One* who can bring streams out of deserts, and fountains out of desolation. Jesus is the Fountain of Living Water.

Transforming Grace

Jesus said to them, "I am the bread of life; he who comes to Me shall not hunger, and he who believes in Me shall never thirst. (John 6:35) Never thirst! If you're spiritually thirsty, it is because somehow you've disconnected from the Supply. The Supply is still there; you need to get connected again. Come to Jesus and let Him flood your life and satisfy the thirst that you have in your heart.

> *How precious is Your lovingkindness, O God! And the children of men take refuge in the shadow of Your wings. They drink their fill of the abundance of Your house; and You give them to drink of the river of Your delights. For*

with You is the fountain of life; in Your light we see light.
(Psalm 36:7-9)

In Christ, we can drink our fill. God offers a boundless supply. What about when you get thirsty again? *Have some more of the water Jesus gives, because it never ends.* Wells may go dry, and cisterns may spring a leak. What this world offers will run out, but God never runs dry. There is always a new supply with the Lord.

Are you facing something that is tremendously difficult? *God will have what you need to face it.* Every day there are new mercies, a new supply of strength, hope and help from God. The fountain is never turned off. In Arizona, they turn off the fountains to conserve water during the hot summer months. In contrast, God is extravagant! We live in a *desert* (the world), but He doesn't turn off His supply to conserve the living water; God's supply will not evaporate. If you have a huge need, God has a huge supply. He doesn't ration the living water. There is plenty, and it will always be available anytime you need it. It is flowing, running, quick and lively. It is abundant living water, because God is the *Fountain* of Life.

When the western United States experiences prolonged drought, people are encouraged to be more careful with their water usage. A few of the ways to conserve water include being very careful not to flush toilets unless absolutely necessary, resisting the temptation to take long, luxurious, showers or letting the faucet run while you wash your hands or brush your teeth. *Our God doesn't ration living water. It's abundant, and it will never, never run dry.*

> *And He said to me, 'It is done. I am the Alpha and the Omega, the beginning and the end. I will give to the one who thirsts from the spring of the water of life without cost. (Revelation 21:6)*

God's supply doesn't cost you anything; you're not going to get a monthly water bill. In Phoenix, summertime water bills can be horrendous. Our family used to have fruit trees and an automatic sprinkler for our lawn. When summer hit and we received the water bills, we would think, *Is this really worth it?* Eventually, we moved and our new home is xeriscaped with desert plants, cactus, and the typical ground cover in our Sonoran desert – rock.

You are never going to get a bill from God for the water that He gives you, because it is free and abundant. It will never be rationed, and it is available for eternity.

> *And the Spirit and the bride say, "Come." And let the one*

Transforming Grace

> *who hears say, "Come." And let the one who is thirsty come; let the one who wishes take the water of life without cost.* (Revelation 22:17)

These are some of the final words that God has given to us in the Bible: *Come! Get a drink! It's without cost. If you're thirsty, I've got what you need and it will never run out. You will never be charged for it. It will never be rationed, and it will be there for ever and ever and ever and ever.* God has the living water we so desperately need for spiritual life and satisfaction.

Transforming Grace

Chapter Four

Grace Reveals the Truth

> *Now on the last day, the great*
> *day of the feast, Jesus stood*
> *and cried out, saying, "If any*
> *man is thirsty…"* (John 7:37)

The background of this verse is interesting. The timing is during the Feast of Sukkot, which is also called the Feast of Tabernacles. The people built temporary shelters (Sukkahs) in and around Jerusalem as part of the celebration for this joyful feast. They camped in their Sukkahs for an entire week. On the last day, the great day of the feast, there was a special ceremony at the Temple. The High Priest, followed by the other priests, Levites and worshippers, carried a golden jar (or a pitcher) as he walked down the southern steps of the temple mount to the farthest southern point of David's city which ended at the Pool of Siloam. The High Priest would fill the golden container with water from the pool, hike to the top of the temple mount and pour the water on the altar. The water ran down the altar while the worshippers waved palm branches and sang the Psalms of Ascent.

The Feast of Tabernacles takes place during early Fall when it is still hot and dry in Israel. Picture yourself as a part of the crowd as you wave palm branches, hike down the mountain to the Pool of Siloam and back up to the Temple Mount, all the while singing loudly. When the High Priest pours the water on the altar, everyone falls silent during this special movement. As you hear the water running down the altar, Jesus stands up and calls out, *Is anyone thirsty?* What a question! *Everyone* is thirsty! Everyone's tongue is swollen in their mouths because they are so thirsty! We've been shouting, singing, waving palm branches and hiking up and down Temple Mount in the hot sun! *YES, we're thirsty!*

Jesus declared:

Transforming Grace

"If any man is thirsty, let him come to Me and drink. He who believes in Me, as the Scripture said, 'From his innermost being shall flow rivers of living water.'" But this He spoke of the Spirit, whom those who believed in Him were to receive; for the Spirit was not yet given, because Jesus was not yet glorified. (John 7:37-39)

Jesus identified the Holy Spirit as the One Who is the River of Living Water. In other words, God, Himself, will indwell us. He will flow from our life, giving us life, refreshing us and flowing out to refresh others.

Transforming Grace

This is the Living Water that Jesus was referring to as He spoke to the Samaritan woman. *I will give you this Living Water - this life-giving, flowing-out-of-your-innermost-being kind of water.*

> *She said to Him, "Sir, You have nothing to draw with..."*
> (John 4:11)

She didn't understand what Jesus meant by "Living Water." She was still thinking of the water in the well. She continued:

> *"Sir, you have nothing to draw with and the well is deep where then do you give that*

> *living water, you are not*
> *greater than our father Jacob*
> *who gave us the well and*
> *drank of it himself and his*
> *sons and his cattle are you?"*
> (John 4:11-12)

Jacob was one of the patriarchs of the Jews and the Samaritans. Centuries before this conversation, Jacob dug the well where the woman and Jesus met. As wonderful a blessing as Jacob's well was to the people, it wasn't Living Water, the flowing springs of life-giving, gushing water that comes from God. It was merely a well. That's all that any man, no matter how great a man he may be, can do - dig a little well.

Transforming Grace

You may have a wonderful spiritual heritage. There may be wells that have been dug for you by spiritual people, but it's not enough. Perhaps your parents, grandparents, teachers or some important person in your life gave you a cup of water and showed you a well; however, you are still spiritually dry. We can't survive on the wonderful people in our past. Their relationship with God will not sustain us. We need to have the life-giving water from Jesus Himself; the relationship that God wants to have with us is a personal relationship between us and Him.

This relationship is not something that can be passed down to us. We don't have a personal relationship with Jesus because someone that we love is close to Him; we can't rub shoulders with them and hope it's going to rub off on us. That's not enough! God doesn't have grandchildren! He has *children.* Jesus is greater than our father Jacob, greater than those wonderful, precious people that God has used to dig wells and bring water to us. Jesus is greater, and He wants us to stop depending on our spiritual heritage and go right to Him, the Source. He wants to give us a personal connection with the Fountain of Living Water and not rely on a spirituality that we have gotten vicariously through someone else. Go right to the Source, and get it right from Jesus.

Transforming Grace

> *"You are not greater than our father Jacob, are You, who gave us the well, and drank of it himself, and his sons, and his cattle?" Jesus answered and said to her, "Everyone who drinks of this water shall thirst again."* (John 4:12-13)

If you're drinking from the wells of other people - even if they are great wells, dug by a mighty person of God - you're going to get thirsty again. You are going to run out.

> *"Everyone who drinks of this water shall thirst again; but whoever drinks of the water that I shall give him shall*

> *never thirst; but the water that I shall give him shall become in him a well of water springing up to eternal life." The woman said to Him, "Sir, give me this water, so I will not be thirsty, nor come all the way here to draw." He said to her, "Go, call your husband, and come here." The woman answered and said, "I have no husband."* (John 4:13-17)

The woman was beginning to feel the conviction of her sin, so she 'reframed' the truth. She wasn't willing to be completely honest about her situation. It was true that she didn't presently have a husband, but only a half-truth. Isn't that the way of human nature when the Lord starts to get hold of us? We are tempted to hedge the truth, aren't we? We may admit a part of the truth, but we're afraid to see the whole truth because we may think God will reject us. The woman had been rejected by everyone; that's why she came at noon to draw water. No one else would be there at that time of day. *She had been rejected! She wasn't about to be rejected again; she was going to protect herself.*

A lot of us have experienced rejection, and, as a result, we build walls around ourselves to protect ourselves from further pain. What happens when we build those walls? In time, the walls get so thick and high that we're isolated, and the pain of being behind those walls is even worse than the pain of being rejected by others.

God wants to come and help us tear down our walls. Yes, we may get rejected by some people, but we will never be rejected by the Lord. He's not *ever* going to turn His back on us and walk away! He encourages us, *I will never leave you or forsake you,*[4] *'All that the Father gives me will come to me, and whoever comes to me I will never cast out.'*[5] He will never reject us.

> *The woman answered and said, "I have no husband."*

---

[4] Hebrews 13:5 (NRSV)
[5] John 6:37 (ESV)

> *Jesus said to her, "You have well said, 'I have no husband'; for you have had five husbands, and the one whom you now have is not your husband; this you have said truly."* (John 4:17-18)

Jesus compassionately met the woman at the point of her fear of disclosure. He didn't condemn her but showed great grace as He helped her transition to a place of complete honesty. He didn't criticize her but simply affirmed the portion of truth she had shared with Him. He said, *'You have spoken the truth.'* Then, He went ahead and revealed the rest of the story.

Transforming Grace

The woman said to Him, "Sir, I perceive that You are a prophet." (John 4:19)

The woman was given spiritual insight at that moment. She understood that the person she was talking to was not an ordinary person because He could look beyond what she shared and know the details of her life. He knew her. Because she realized He was a prophet, she opened up and asked the questions that had been filling her heart: *How can I worship God? How can I get close to God? I'm confused. Our fathers say one thing, the Jews say another, and I feel so far away from God that I'm probably a hopeless case anyway.* The cry of her heart was: *I want to worship God; I want to be close to God.*

> *The woman said to Him, "Sir,
> I perceive that You are a
> prophet." Our fathers
> worshiped in this mountain,
> and you people say that in
> Jerusalem is the place where
> men ought to worship." Jesus
> said to her, "Woman, believe
> Me, an hour is coming when
> neither in this mountain nor
> in Jerusalem will you worship
> the Father. You worship what
> you do not know..."* (John
> 4:19-22)

They didn't know all of the truth because
the Samaritans only had the first five
books of the Bible. They didn't have the

rest of the Old Testament: the prophetic writings, the historical books, or the Psalms - only Genesis, Exodus, Leviticus, Numbers, and Deuteronomy.

> *"You worship that which you do not know; we worship that which we know, for salvation is from the Jews. But an hour is coming, and now is, when the true worshipers shall worship the Father in spirit and truth; for such people the Father seeks to be His worshipers."* (John 4:22-23)

This is amazing! Jesus told her, *Listen, I know your heart. You want to be close to God; you want to worship God? God is looking for you; He's seeking you. You don't need to worship in a holy place because God is standing right in front of you. The hour has come that worshipping God is a matter of the heart. You have a holy temple of God in your heart, and you can worship God in spirit and in truth.*

We worship with the Word of God through the Holy Spirit of God. True worship is not something that we do in a special building, a holy location or a temple. We, who believe in Jesus, are the temple of God. We worship God all the time. Everywhere we go we take the temple with us, because God indwells us.

Transforming Grace

If you take a trip to Israel, God is not closer there than He is right where you live. Even though you may feel like you are closer to God if you go to the top of a mountain, God is still with you in the valley. God is with us everywhere. We worship in spirit and in truth. The time of meeting God in a special holy temple has passed. God is Spirit, and those who worship Him do not have to worship Him in holy places, only in spirit and truth. Grace reveals the truth about how to worship God.

> *The woman said to Him, "I know that Messiah is coming (He who is called Christ); when that One comes, He will*

declare all things to us." (John 4:25)

What she was actually asking was, *Are you the Messiah?*

Jesus then gave her a stupendous revelation of Himself. It was a revelation that, as we have already seen, had not been given to anyone else on the earth living at that time. He said to her,

> *"I who speak to you am He."*
> (John 4:26)

The English translation of Jesus' words is not completely adequate; it's even more powerful if you <u>literally</u> translate the original Greek: *"It is I AM who speaks to you."*

Now, she would have known who *I AM* was, because that's the name that God gave when He revealed Himself to her ancestor Moses at the burning bush. She was acquainted with that name for God - *I AM that I am.* Jesus said, *"It is I AM who speaks to you."*

He proclaimed Himself as the I AM! *I AM Jehovah. I AM the Almighty God. I AM the One at the burning bush. I AM the One who led your ancestors, the Jews, out of slavery, bondage, oppression and rejection into abundance, to the river of Living Water and to the Promised Land. It is I AM who speaks to you.*

I can't even imagine what her response must have been. Here was the *I AM*, that consuming fire that did not consume, the burning bush, the One before whom Moses, that man of God, had to take off his sandals, because he was standing on holy ground. In contrast, here she was: a sinful, despised, Samaritan woman standing before the great I AM of eternity. Grace reveals that Jesus is God, but He is not out to destroy us. He is out to bless us!

Transforming Grace

Chapter Five

Grace Gives Us a Mission

While Jesus revealed He was the *I AM* to the woman, His disciples walked up at that moment of truth. They marveled that He had been speaking with a woman, because that's not something that they would have done. God always surprises us; He acts in ways that we wouldn't expect. He is not constrained by our expectations, and there isn't a 'box' that can contain Him. *"Yet, no one said to her, 'What do you seek?' And none of them said to Him, 'Why do you speak with her?'"* (John 4:27) They came up to Jesus and the woman with the food they had bought in the village - Samaritan 'take out.' They may have been thinking, *All right, we've got the food! We've got what everybody needs.* But, when they saw Jesus talking to the woman, they may have thought, *Why is He doing that?* It didn't even cross their minds to ask her, *What do you need'* or to ask Jesus: *What are You talking about? Why are You talking to her?* Their priorities were awry, and all they could focus on was their empty stomachs.

Like the disciples, how many times have we missed incredible opportunities because our focus was on our needs and priorities? The disciples were hungry and thirsty. They needed to eat, but their empty stomachs weren't *the* most important thing.

Oh, may the Lord give us a heart that goes for the most important priorities, so that we perceive God's agenda. God will take care of all our needs. He knows we have need of things to wear, places to live and things to eat and drink. He knows our needs. *"Seek first His kingdom and His righteousness and all these things,* (these 'things' of the flesh that we need) *will be added unto you."* (Matthew 6:33) The disciples focused only on their fleshly needs, and it didn't occur to them to ask what was going on, even though they were curious! The situation seemed strange to them, but they kept silent.

Transforming Grace

So the woman left her water pot. (John 4:28)

She didn't leave her water pot because it was too heavy to carry back to the city, or because she was in a hurry. She didn't need her water pot (in a spiritual sense) anymore because she had the Fountain of Living Water. She had come to faith in her Messiah, the *I AM*, and so she left her water pot. She didn't need to draw from the dusty old well anymore because she had the Fountain of Life within. She hurried into the city where the Living Water flowed out of her.

> *The woman left her water pot, and went into the city, and said to the men, "Come, see a*

*man who told me all the
things that I have done; this is
not the Christ, is it?"* (John
4:28-29)

The woman was on a grace mission! She
didn't need to give a Bible study or
explain that Jesus was the Messiah
because she had an awesome testimony.
All she had to do was to go and say,
*Come see somebody; He knows all about me,
and He still loves and accepts me. Is this the
Christ?* Like the woman, we don't have
to have all the answers to be an effective
witness for Jesus. She didn't have a Bible
lesson when she went into town. She
didn't try to explain the prophecies that
pointed forward to Messiah. She just
went into the city and said, *"He told me*

everything about myself." That's all it took. The people in the city were intrigued by her story. *If somebody can tell you all about you, I want to go see this person myself,* they may have thought. They all flocked out of the city to see Jesus because she asked them: *Is this the Messiah?* She didn't know very much, except that Jesus knew about her. He'd accepted her. She had the Living Water!

Like this woman, we can be effective witnesses. Sometimes we feel afraid to share Jesus because we think we don't know enough of the Bible. We think that we've got to have all the answers. *I can never say anything because I don't know the Bible.* Some of God's most effective witnesses didn't know much other than they knew their need for God's help, and that God had come to their rescue.

You can be an effective witness. You don't have to possess an extensive Bible knowledge. You don't have to be afraid that someone will ask the question that you can't answer. Effective witnessing is just sharing... *'He helped me. I haven't figured it all out yet, but He did it. Go talk to Him; I know He'll help you, too!'*

> *They went out of the city, and were coming to Him. In the meanwhile, the disciples were requesting Him, saying, "Rabbi, eat." But He said to them, "I have food to eat that you do not know about." The*

> *disciples therefore were saying to one another, "No one brought Him anything to eat, did he?"* (John 4:30-33)

The clueless disciples were puzzled. They asked, *Did somebody sneak out here with a sack lunch when we weren't watching?* We can't be too hard on the disciples because, how many times have we been clueless? I certainly don't know what God is doing all of the time. I know He's doing something, but I haven't figured it out. When I am clueless, does Jesus reject me? Does He scold, *'When are you going to understand?'* Not at all! He draws me to Himself and continues to patiently guide and instruct me.

Transforming Grace

The disciples urged, *'Lunch... You need lunch! Come on and eat!'* Jesus responded, *'I have food and you don't know about it.'* The bewildered disciples asked each other, *'Did He have something to eat?'*

> *And He answered and said to them, "My food is to do the will of Him who sent Me, and to accomplish His work.* (John 4:34)

The most satisfying meal is not a physical one but one which is spiritual. It is much more fulfilling to experience God's food! The satisfaction and excitement you feel when you see that God has used you to speak the Word of

God to someone, to encourage someone in the Lord, to lead someone to Christ or to plant seeds in their life that God will use cannot possibly be compared to a physical meal.   Jesus turned the disciples' attention away from their lunch by explaining, *'My food is not this takeout you brought Me from Sychar; My food is doing the will of God.'*

> *Do you not say, 'There are yet four months, and then comes the harvest'? Behold, I say to you, lift up your eyes, and look on the fields, that they are white for harvest.* (John 4:35)

As Jesus and His disciples looked toward the city of Sychar, their gaze fell on the fields between themselves and the city. The fields of grain were not white for harvest, for the harvest season was still four months away. Rather, it was all of the people who were coming from Sychar to see Jesus. Most of them wore white clothing, and in the shimmering heat, they appeared as a field of ripened grain. Jesus took that moment to teach His disciples a very important lesson: God's grace turns our attention away from ourselves and sends us on a mission. The need of that particular moment was not to eat lunch, but to reach out with God's grace to spiritually hungry people.

> *Already he who reaps is receiving wages, and is*

gathering fruit for life eternal;
that he who sows and he who
reaps may rejoice together.
For in this case the saying is
true, 'One sows, and another
reaps.' I sent you to reap that
for which you have not
labored; others have labored,
and you have entered into
their labor. (John 4:36-38)

Jesus planted the truth in the heart of the Samaritan woman, and she carried the seed of truth and shared it with the men in Sychar. The disciples had not participated in the evangelization of the Samaritans, but they would get to share in helping bring the good news to the people of Sychar. *Okay disciples, you get to enter into this; you get to reap even though you didn't do any of the sowing or any of the preparation. You will get the joy of reaping,* Jesus instructed them.

God graciously grants us the privilege of participating in bringing people to Jesus! Grace has given us a mission. Paul talked about this when he said, *I planted, Apollos watered, but God was causing the growth.* (1 Corinthians 3:6) It is quite common for God to use *many* people to bring the truth to *one* person. In this way, all the praise goes to God; all the glory goes to the Lord.

There are times when we just sow seeds of the Word into people's lives, and we don't see the harvest. There are other times when we come along and have the privilege of leading someone to Jesus. We had nothing to do with the preparation other people did in that person's life before we came along. We just happened to be there at the right time when they were ready to receive Jesus Christ, and we get the joy of seeing them become a Christian. That's what Jesus was teaching His disciples: *Hey, you guys have been all concerned with flesh needs; all you could think about was getting some food.* God doesn't exclude us from participating in the harvest because we haven't had a part in the planting of truth. Rather, His grace is amazingly inclusive and He invites us to share in the joy of seeing people's lives transformed.

And from that city many of the Samaritans believed in Him because of the word of the woman who testified, "He told me all the things that I have done." So when the Samaritans came to Him, they were asking Him to stay with them; and He stayed there two days.   And many more believed because of His word; and they were saying to the woman, "It is no longer because of what you said that we believe, for we have heard for ourselves and know that this One is indeed the Savior of the world." (John 4:39-42)

All we have to do is turn people's attention to Jesus. Initially, they may only be interested in Jesus because of what He has done for us. We share, *God worked in my life; this is what He did,* but our goal is not to draw their attention to ourselves. Rather, our goal is to point them to Jesus so that they no longer believe because of what we have said, but because they see and understand how much He cares for them. Parenting is a great example of this principle. We only have our children for a little while, and that time is given to us so that we can plant the Word of God in them. Our goal is to get their hand into the hand of Jesus so that they will trust Him the rest of their lives. We cannot always be there for them, but Jesus will be there. Their faith and their life cannot be grounded on us but it must be grounded on Him. We've led them to Jesus, but He's the One who will take them all the way through the rest of their lives.

For our friends and for our family our mission is to help point them to Jesus. If we just help them look to Jesus, He'll take care of the rest. They don't have to understand everything, and they may not even believe in Jesus at first. We can get them to look in the right direction, however, and then Jesus will get hold of them.

Point your friends and family towards Jesus, and plant seeds in their life by sharing what God has done for you. Get them aimed towards Jesus, and He will do the rest. Grace gives us a mission!

Chapter Six

Grace for Our Shame

Shame affects all of us to some degree or another. When we think of our past, we may have experiences and choices that we regret. We may feel a sense of shame for what we've done. Shame finds a foothold early in life. It doesn't really matter whether you had a church upbringing, only attended church on Christmas and Easter or you knew nothing about God. Whatever our faith, or lack of it, when we reflect on our past, there are choices we have made and actions we have taken about which we think, *Oh! I wish I hadn't done that! If anyone knew what I have done, what my life has been like and where I've been, they might not like or accept me. God has probably rejected me as well.* To some degree, every individual deals with shame.

I was one of those kids who was blessed by being taken to church every week, and having the values and truths of the Bible impressed on my young mind. I *knew* the Ten Commandments, let me tell you, and I can remember them to this day. I was taught the way we are supposed to live and what is right and wrong. Yet, even in that high moral environment, I still did things that I knew I shouldn't have done.

Transforming Grace

My dad was a logger. He was actually a heavy equipment operator for a logging company, running a bulldozer and the high lead logging tower. During the summers, one of the fun things that we did as a family was to camp near my dad's jobsite in the Trinity Alps mountain range in Northern California. We slept in tents, and Mom cooked with a cast iron kettle on a fire and a two-burner butane stove. My brother and I played with the other kids and swam in a nearby river.

One summer, when I was eight or nine years old, my girlfriend and I spent long hours playing with Barbie dolls. She had the 'coolest' Barbie stuff! It was actually 'store-bought!' How I envied all her doll clothes and accessories. Her Barbies had brightly colored paisley culotte pantsuits and the latest short, short skirts with knee-high white boots. I loved those Barbie clothes. As the summer progressed, however, I wasn't having as much fun playing with her. I was thinking, *I'm going to have to go back home, and I won't get to play with all this great Barbie stuff.* I began to covet her Barbie outfits and accessories.

Now, I was a good little church girl. I knew the eighth commandment, **Thou shalt not steal,** but it didn't help me from wanting her dolls' things. Thus, on the last day we were playing Barbies, when she wasn't looking, I took one of her Barbie's dresses. Now, you may be thinking, *That's a silly, insignificant thing. Everyone makes childish mistakes.* When you are a little kid and you know better, however, it is a huge dilemma. I hid the Barbie dress in my own Barbie case and took it home. While I had that pink polka-dotted dress the entire school year, playing Barbies wasn't fun any longer. In fact, I started playing Barbies in my closet because I was afraid my Mom would find out. She might ask me, *Where did you get this dress?* So I hid in my closet and played alone, feeling miserable, ashamed, and guiltier as the months crept on. I couldn't wait for the next summer when I could return that Barbie outfit and say, *I'm so sorry I stole this dress. Would you please forgive me?*

Transforming Grace

When the Barbie dress was finally returned, I did feel relieved, yet, at the same time, I continued to carry the shame of that experience. Even though I knew my friend forgave me, and God forgave me, there was something unsettling about it that attached itself to me. That something was **shame.** Although I was only a child, I felt a deep sense of shame for the first time. *If people knew what I had done, they wouldn't want anything to do with me. I'm so ashamed!* The humiliation and embarrassment that I experienced was so real and tangible, that it seemed to me that everyone could see the shame hanging around my neck. It was like wearing a lanyard with a name tag attached on which was written

S-H-A-M-E in large letters for everyone to read.

As time went by, I collected other shame lanyards. When I hit my teen years and mouthed off at my parents, I knew better than that! Even though they forgave me, I still felt ashamed. I was the good girl, and I wasn't supposed to say things like that with such a disrespectful attitude. Other 'shame lanyards' found their way around my neck. I began dating in those years. Even with my church attendance and moral training, I occasionally let myself step across relational boundaries that were too intimate for that time in my life. I was well on my way to having a large shame collection hanging around my neck.

You may think, *Those are little things! They are not that evil!* But, those 'little things' were very shameful to me, because I was religious. I knew right from wrong, and I deliberately chose to do what I knew was wrong. I was ashamed of the way I had lived and the choices I had made. I was ashamed of my mistakes and my failures.

The degree of our sin, how bad it may be as rated by ourselves or others, is not really that critical when we are considering the shame we feel for our sin. We all collect shame, whether we are a moral person (as others judge us), or someone who has really blown it (as we may assess ourselves). Shamecollecting is universal. It's hard to detach from the shame that hangs around our necks. Even if you are a Christian and you have experienced grace and forgiveness, you can still struggle with a lingering sense of shame, because *shame* is not the same thing as *guilt*. When we have received and accepted forgiveness, the guilt for what we have done drops away. The shame we feel, however, may continue to weigh us down.

Shame can accompany guilt, but they are entirely different:

- *Guilt* is the conviction that 'I've <u>done</u> something wrong.' It's a wonderful gift that God gives to help point us in the right direction, and to bring us to the place of saying, "Lord, I'm sorry! I was wrong. Please forgive me." We can also make that kind of apology to others when necessary. Guilt is a gift because it points out our sin and prompts us to seek forgiveness.

- *Shame* is entirely different from guilt. Shame involves feelings of self-loathing, embarrassment, fear of being exposed (hiding in the closet to avoid being found out), and trying to cover up. It's not just our knowing that we have <u>made</u> a mistake; it's our belief that we **are** the mistake. That's the difference; shame identifies us by our sin. Shame is the self-talk that goes something like this: *If people really knew me and they knew what I have done, they wouldn't want anything to do with me.*

I had started to think of myself as a thief, a bad person, as I looked at myself through the prism of my failures and mistakes. In time, those shame-filled thoughts became my identity; they became the way I viewed myself.

My husband often says, *I love it when people come into the church, and they say, 'I am an alcoholic,' (and they are a Christian).* He enjoys telling them, *You are **not** an alcoholic when you are a Christian. You are* *a man or a woman in Christ.*[6] God doesn't look at you and say, *Oh! You are a horrible alcoholic!* The rest of your life you don't have to affirm an incorrect identity by saying,

- I'm an alcoholic
- I'm an adulterer
- I'm a murderer
- I'm a thief
- I'm a cheat
- I'm a gossip
- I'm a backbiter

Whatever issues have caused us to feel shame in our life, our sin, mistakes and failures do not define us. Our sin is not

---

[6] Used by permission. Pastor J. Mark Martin, Calvary Community Church, Phoenix, Arizona

our identity. God sees us through eyes of love and grace, and there is no shame.

Lets' take a look at the origin of shame as spoken of in the first book of the Bible, the book of Genesis. Then, we're going to turn to the New Testament and look at another example of shame in the Scripture. It's appropriate to go to Genesis, the book of beginnings, to find the origin of shame because shame got its hold on people at the beginning. When God created Adam and Eve, they were completely whole and perfect, without any hint of shame.

> *And the man and his wife were both naked and were not ashamed.* (Genesis 2:25)

Transforming Grace

The nakedness of Adam and Eve didn't cause them to feel ashamed. In fact, they were completely comfortable and transparent with each other. They didn't hide anything from each other or from God. They were perfect, because God had made everything good, including them. When they ate from the fruit of the tree of the knowledge of good and evil, however, they began to have a disturbing self-awareness. All of a sudden, they acquired the self-awareness that they were dirty in some way. For the first time, they realized that they were naked, and they looked for ways to cover themselves. They felt ashamed and naked. They were literally attacked by shame. They were the only two people on the planet, and they were ashamed. That's pretty sad, isn't it?

As a kid, I collected dolls. Dolls that had belonged to my Mom and to my grandparents were all lined up on the shelves in my room with all of the other dolls I had collected. At one point, as I was getting a little older (around junior high age), I started freaking out because of all those eyes looking at me. I wonder whether that's similar to Adam and Eve's experience. They were the only two people on earth, but were they uncomfortable with the giraffes and the monkeys looking at their nakedness? *Oh, we're so ashamed!* They realized that they were naked, and they felt exposed, embarrassed and uncomfortable with themselves, and with each other. The Bible goes on to say that they sewed fig leaves together and made 'clothing' for themselves.

> *Then the eyes of both of them were opened, and they knew that they were naked; and they sewed fig leaves together and made themselves loin coverings.* (Genesis 3:7)

We used to have a fig tree in our yard. After picking figs and brushing against fig leaves, I've come to the realization that you or I would have to be completely desperate to wear fig leaves, because they are extremely irritating when your skin brushes up against them.

Transforming Grace

Can you imagine wearing fig leaves? How in the world did they sew leaves together for their loin coverings (literally 'aprons')? These were desperate people! Very desperate! They reached for the first thing they could find to try to cover up, because they were overcome with shame. From that point on, they couldn't be who they were created to be. Shame is at the root of all our efforts to conceal ourselves from others. We're afraid of people knowing the real 'us.' We pretend to be something that deep down we believe we really aren't. We don't let people in; we don't let them know our past, our struggles, and the awful things we have done.

*They heard the sound of the
LORD God walking in the
garden in the cool of the day,
and the man and his wife hid
themselves from the presence
of the LORD God among the
trees of the garden. Then the
LORD God called to the man,
and said to him, "Where are
you?" He said, "I heard the
sound of You in the garden,
and I was afraid because I was
naked; so I hid myself."*
(Genesis 3:8-10)

Why did they hide? They hid because of
fear and shame. They had never
experienced the fear of self-disclosure.
Before they ate from the tree of

knowledge, their relationship with each other and with God was that of total love, acceptance, intimacy and transparency, but shame motivated them to cover up. Shame compelled them to run and hide. Shame is still one of Satan's most powerful tools to drive us away from God, and from each other. *Cover up! Run! Hide! Don't let anyone know who you really are!* We cry out, "I've done something disgusting!" And Satan whispers, "You ***are*** something disgusting!"

That's shame.

Transforming Grace

Chapter Seven

Grace Takes Away Our Shame

Now that we have looked at the origin of shame, let's consider another type of shame. As we've already seen in the previous chapter, there is the shame that we deal with in our own lives in how we talk to ourselves about the things that we have done, our feelings of inadequacy or fear of being exposed. I think that would be enough shame in a person's life! Unfortunately, we also often have to deal with the shame of what others say and do *to* us.

Perhaps you grew up in an alcoholic family. *You* weren't the one who drank themselves silly every weekend, came home and beat up or tried to kill one of your family members. *You* weren't the one to waste all the family money. *You* didn't do that! *You* didn't break every promise that was made by failing to show up at your child's high school graduation, wedding or other important event in their life. *You* didn't do that! *You* weren't the alcoholic; nevertheless, what do you carry? You carry *shame* from growing up in that family, and the shame that the alcoholic put on you and the rest of the family as they transferred their responsibility and blame-shifted everyone else. Maybe, you were the one who was molested as a child. *You* were not the criminal, but you've been made to feel ashamed of what was done to you. It seems like it would be enough to just feel ashamed for what we do ourselves without having the shame of what others do placed on us, doesn't it?

A humorous story I once read provides a good illustration of this type of shame. Some children at a parochial school were having a hard time remembering their sins when it was time to go into the confessional. Their teachers, therefore, instructed them to write down their sins before they went in. One little second-grade boy did as he was told and then went into the booth and sat down. He heard the voice behind the screen quietly

ask, *What do you have to confess, my son?*
He started to read his little list:

- I lied to my parents
- I disobeyed my Mom
- I fought with my brothers and...
  WAIT A MINUTE! This isn't even my list!"

Can you relate? Do you feel shamed by someone else? It's not uncommon to collect shame from others as we are around them. We wear shame lanyards of things that have been done <u>to</u> us, as well as the shame we feel for our own actions. The Apostle John records a poignant story of a woman who experienced both kinds of shame.

But Jesus went to the Mount of Olives. Early in the morning He came again into the temple, and all the people were coming to Him; and He sat down and began to teach them. The scribes and the Pharisees brought a woman caught in adultery, and having set her in the center of the court, they said to Him, "Teacher, this woman has been caught in adultery, in the very act."Now in the Law Moses commanded us to stone such women; what then do You say?" They were saying this, testing Him, so that they might have grounds for

> *accusing Him. But Jesus*
> *stooped down and with His*
> *finger wrote on the ground.*
> (John 8:1-6)

This is appalling! I'm not referring to the actions of this woman, although what she did was wrong. More shocking than her actions were those of the scribes and the Pharisees; they were supposed to be religious leaders! They were entrusted to be the compassionate shepherds, wise leaders and faithful teachers of the people. They were men who should have had love and compassion for all people, including this woman. They should have expended every effort to help her understand God's Word and to experience His love, so she wouldn't feel compelled to look for it somewhere else. Instead of helping, teaching, shepherding, guarding, guiding, leading and protecting, they shamed her! They simply didn't care about her. She was a pawn in their game. Their goal was to set a trap for Jesus and she was the bait. The pious religious leaders were consumed with jealousy and hatred for Christ. They would go to any lengths to discredit Him, to arrest Him, to bring Him to trial and execution and to divert the loyalty of the people from Him. It absolutely did not matter to them who they used and abused along the way. This woman's mistake conveniently provided a perfect opportunity for them to launch their diabolical, hateful plan.

The adultery must have been a setup, because how else would they have 'happened' to discover her in the very act? *Where's the guy?* Adultery isn't a solitary sin! The Law actually said that if a man and a woman were caught in the act of adultery, if there was the testimony of two or three reliable witnesses, then *both* of them were to be executed.

We are told that the scribes and the Pharisees *brought her to Jesus.* That sounds rather tame, as though they had said to her, *Come along now - we're going to take you to Jesus.* That's not at all what the word means in the Greek text. The

word is *'kateileemmeneen'*[7] and it means
"to take eagerly; to seize and drag
someone." They knew just when to rush
into that bedroom, seize her and drag
her out in public and into the temple
courts. Who knows what she may have
been able to grab to throw around
herself as they were forcing her out of
the room while they piously intoned
their accusations against her! They
couldn't wait to push her half-naked
body in front of Jesus.

Such women should be stoned! The Greek
word used for 'such women' means
women of this sort. This **kind** of woman!
In other words, *She's not even a normal*

---

[7] John 8:3…*kateileemmeneen* (from Interlinear Transliterated
Bible, Copyright 1994, 2003 by Biblesoft, Inc.)

woman! She's not someone that you should value as a person! She was one of *those* women: hopeless, detestable, disgusting, evil, filthy, and dirty. The self-righteous leaders utterly distained her.

Such women...*should be stoned according to the Law.*

> **Shame** *on you, woman!*

> **Shame** *on you!*

> **Shame** *on you!*

Can you hear the accusation in their voices? Can you imagine the shame lanyards being hung around her neck?

Transforming Grace

But Jesus stooped down and with His finger wrote on the ground. But when they persisted in asking Him, He straightened up, and said to them, 'He, who is without sin among you, let him be the first to throw a stone at her.' Again He stooped down and wrote on the ground. When they heard it, they began to go out one by one, beginning with the older ones, and He was left alone, and the woman, where she was, in the center of the court. (John 8:6b-9)

Transforming Grace

The Law commanded the death penalty for adultery. The woman was guilty, but the self-righteous accusers that publicly dragged her out into the temple courts, while loudly asserting their righteousness and her guilt, were also guilty. No one has the right to point the finger at someone else.

> *What a **shameful** sinner she is…*
> *What an **awful** man he is…*
> *What a **hopeless** case she is…*

Jesus stooped down and began writing on the ground with His finger. It's a real 'God' thing to write with your finger. In fact, God wrote with His finger when He gave the Law, didn't He? *Ok, talk to Me about the Law,* Jesus was saying, *I'm the*

One who wrote it, and He started writing on the ground. When God gave the Law, He wrote it in stone. When God wrote on the ground, He wrote it in the dust.

> *O LORD, the hope of Israel, all who forsake You will be put to shame. Those who turn away on earth will be written down, because they have forsaken the fountain of living water, even the LORD.*
> (Jeremiah 17:13)

This verse describes those unbelieving scribes and Pharisees, doesn't it? They didn't love Jesus! They had forsaken the true and living God and would not accept His Son, the Messiah, who was right in front of them. Because they rejected the One that God sent, their names were written in the dust. Maybe it was the names of those self-righteous scribes and Pharisees that Jesus inscribed in the dust because they rejected Him as the Lord, the *Fountain of Living Water.*

A few moments after Jesus started writing, the only one left with the woman was the only One righteous enough to throw a stone, Jesus, Himself. *Jesus said to her, 'Woman, where are they? Did no one condemn you?' And she said, 'No one, Lord.' And Jesus said, 'Neither do I condemn you; go your way: From now on sin no more.'* (John 8:10-11) This is powerful! Jesus did not condemn the adulterous woman standing in front of Him, and neither does God condemn us! *There is therefore now no condemnation to those who are in Christ Jesus.*[8] He doesn't drag us in front of a jeering crowd and shout, **Shame on you!** God will never do that to you; He doesn't condemn you. The only One who has the right to condemn you won't do it if you put your trust in His Son, Jesus Christ, and accept His forgiveness and the gift of salvation.

How could Jesus forgive the adulterous woman and release her from her guilt *and* shame? It was because He would not only pay the price for her guilt by dying in her place, but He would also pay the price for her shame. He died for

---

[8] Romans 8:11 (NASB)

her guilt *and* for her shame. There are those of us who believe we are forgiven and set free from our condemnation and guilt, but we still carry shame. How can we be released from the *shame* of what we've done? We need emancipation from the tyranny of shame. If you are carrying shame for what you have done, you can bring that shame to Jesus. He died to take away your guilt and your shame.

On the cross, Jesus died and shed his blood for the forgiveness of our sin and for our release from guilt and condemnation before God. However, there are all sorts of things that Jesus suffered in addition to shedding His blood to forgive us and take away our guilt. These other things that were done to Him have everything to do with taking on the *shame* of our sins. Jesus not only took our guilt, but He took our shame.

When Adam and Eve sinned, what did they realize? What did they feel? They realized that they were naked! Their nakedness was a part of their shame. How did Jesus die on the cross? He was naked. As He hung on the cross, the scene wasn't like those beautiful paintings that show a cloth modestly covering His loins. There was nothing covering Jesus. He didn't even have a scratchy fig apron! He hung naked and exposed in the full shame of the cross, because He was taking our shame for us.

Did He have to die *naked* to pay the price for our sin? *No!* He simply had to die for our sin and shed His blood. He was stripped because he took our shame. He took our feelings of humiliation, embarrassment and fear of exposure.

Let's look further at the Bible's account of Jesus taking our shame. People humiliated Jesus. They pulled out his beard and spit in His face. Did He need to have someone spit in His face in order to pay the price for our salvation? *No!* But that was the practice at that period of history and in that culture to shame someone. You spit at them. Jesus took the spit! They dressed Him in a king's robe and shoved a crown of thorns on His head. They grabbed a reed, stuck it in His hand and bowed down to Him mocking, *Hail, 'King of the Jews,'* before they led Him out to be crucified. They paraded Him through the streets of Jerusalem as a condemned criminal in front of a jeering crowd. Did He need to experience this humiliation to save us? No, salvation's only requirement was His life, the shedding of His blood in our place. He chose to accept the abuse; the shame, for us.

> *And the people passing by shouted abuse, shaking their heads in mockery. 'So! You can destroy the Temple and build again in three days, can you? Well then, if you are the Son of God, save yourself and*

come down from the cross!'
(Matthew 27:39-40)

While Jesus hung on the cross, the bystanders shamed Him. Oh, the humiliation of it all! He was hanging there naked for us, and no one stood up for Him, spoke encouragement or tried to comfort Him. Instead, they derided, *"**If** you are the Son of God, come down from the cross." Oh! You think you're so great? Shame on you! Shame on you! Shame on you!*

> *The leading priests, the teachers of religious law, and the other leaders also mocked Jesus. "He saved others," they scoffed, "but he can't save*

*himself! So he is the king of
Israel, is he? Let him come
down from the cross, and we
will believe in him! He trusted
God – let God show his
approval by delivering him!
For he said, 'I am the Son of
God.'" And the criminals who
were crucified with him also
shouted the same insults at
him.* (Matthew 27:41-44)

Why would Jesus be abused and
mocked, scoffed at, insulted and
humiliated when all that was required
for our forgiveness was His death and
the shedding of His blood? Why is this
detail included in the gospel accounts?
Jesus only had to die for our sins and

wash away our guilt by His blood, but God's grace goes beyond the needs of forgiveness and the cleansing of our guilt. Jesus also takes away our shame! He took the shame, the abuse, the spitting, the mocking, the nakedness and the insults for us, so that we don't have to feel any hint of shame. He not only released us from our guilt, but He took away all our shame as well. It was all done on that cross for us.

He took our shame.

This is the end of shame.

Chapter Eight

Living in Grace

We've considered the powerful, amazing grace of God in meeting us unexpectedly at the most desperate point of our life, the grace of God that saves us and the grace of God that releases us from our shame. In this last chapter, let's look at how we can experience God's grace every day of our life. Generally, Christians have a good understanding that grace is the basis of salvation, grace opens heaven's doors and grace releases us from guilt and condemnation. We have a natural tendency, however, to move on from this understanding of grace. We begin to live as though God is grading our performance. We start thinking, perhaps, that God (or some other person) is disappointed in us when we fail to achieve certain standards and expectations. We may find it easy to begin our Christian life in grace, but then we slip into a graceless routine. How can we continue to live in God's grace, applying it to every facet of our lives?

There is an incredible beauty and freedom depicted in ballet. I love the moment when the male dancer sweeps the ballerina off her feet and holds her above his head as he carries her across the stage. As the music swells to a crescendo of joy and exuberance, it appears as if she is merely as weightless as a feather. As I've watched, there is something inside me that longs to dance, to float, to soar and to be able to do all those things that I can't physically do.

There's something deep down inside all of us that longs to experience the dance of grace with God. He is that strong dancer that carries us through life. For many of us, however, life is anything but a dance. We don't feel the freedom. Instead of being lifted up, we're crushed with difficulties. Have you ever wondered why the Christian life seems so hard? *"It just doesn't seem to work for me. Jesus loves me, **but**...!"* Have you ever added that little *'but'* in there? "It seems to work for you, **but** *I'm not a very good Christian."* Have you noticed, that when you mention your past or your present spiritual condition, you sound apologetic? Are you still feeling guilty or ashamed?

One evening, some of my friends and I were reminiscing about our weddings. Now, you would think that weddings would be a fun topic for discussion between friends! It seems that we girls start talking about weddings as soon as we are able to talk. We make our scrapbooks with all the pictures we've cut out from the bridal magazines, and our ideas develop throughout our teen years until we actually say, *I do!* But, that evening when we were discussing our weddings, one of my very dear friends hung her head and apologetically said, *I feel so bad. We were just married in Las Vegas.* Although she was unaware, I was thinking, *You got married! That's the important thing! You are still married and you love the Lord and each other. Who cares about the fact that your wedding was in Las Vegas?*

It's so easy to fall into the legalistic trap of berating ourselves for not achieving some standard we, or others, have set. Sometimes, we sound apologetic for our lives. We feel guilty and ashamed. If we were brave enough to admit it, in those quiet, lonely times, late at night we muse, *Why don't I experience the abundant life? I know I'm saved, but my life is just kind of a blah-life, a hard life, or a 'sludge-through-the-peanut-butter' kind of life.*

Transforming Grace

*Where is the **abundant** life of freedom?* What we are going to look at next has the power to transform the way we think, the way we view our Christian lives, and the way we live. Right now, we can experience joy, excitement, exuberance, total love and acceptance. We can feel encouraged, loved and supported by God every day of our lives.

> *The steps of the godly are directed by the LORD.* ***He delights in every detail of their lives.*** (Psalms 37:23)

God delights in us! Read that again, God delights in us. You may find that hard to accept so let's try making it a little more personal. Read this out loud, *God delights in me.* Is that still hard to grasp? Let's put your name in there and make it your own personal declaration. *God delights in <u>(Your Name)</u>!* That's right. God delights in *you*!

How many of us really experience that truth on a daily basis? When we wake up in the morning is our first thought, *"God delights in me?"* Well, maybe after our first cup of coffee we can think, *"God delights in me!"* For some of us, after our first diet Pepsi we remember, *"God delights in me!"* I don't know about you, but most of the time I'm not thinking that God delights in me, because there is this little voice in my head (I'd like to silence it!) that keeps telling me how awful I am. It tells me how ill-equipped

I am for life, and that I am a miserable failure.

The Bible says that God **delights** in us! Now, most English translations use the word *'delights,'* but there are some translations that read, *God is* **pleased** *with us.* That doesn't quite convey the same thing to me! *'Pleased'* is only an *okay* word. I'm glad that God is pleased rather than displeased with me, but it sounds formal. *'Pleased'* is controlled and calm. I think of it as a response to my doing something that prompts God to be happy with me. *Oh, I'm so pleased with you; you did a good job!* My parents were *pleased* when I came home with a good report card. Of course, I didn't show them the ones that weren't good, because I wanted them to always be pleased with me. My piano teacher was *pleased* with me if I could perform well. That word, *pleased*, is all about **me**. It's about performance; doing it beautifully, flawlessly and without mistakes. Don't you agree the word *delights* is more specific and encouraging than the word *pleased?* In my opinion, it is far better than *pleased*!

Someone might counter, *My version says that God delights in the **good** or **godly** man's steps. How could God delight in someone who is living less than a godly life? How do you respond to that?* Well, if God is only delighted with the good and godly people, then all of us might as well give up our hope of God's love and acceptance. There is not a single one of us that is good or godly enough. The only way to be godly in God's sight is to be covered with the goodness of Jesus Christ. When we accept Jesus, God views us as perfect because of Jesus, not because of our stellar lives! *As the Scriptures say, "No one is good - not even one. No one has real understanding; no one is seeking God. All have turned away from God; all have gone wrong.*[9] (Romans 3:10-12) No one is righteous - not anyone. God isn't delighted with us because we're godly. He's delighted with us because we're in His Son. We're godly because of Jesus.

---

[9] *Holy Bible, New Living Translation* ®, copyright © 1996, 2004 by Tyndale Charitable Trust. Used by permission of Tyndale House Publishers. All rights reserved.

Well, I still don't think God delights in me! I'm always messing up. God's delight is not founded on my performing well, getting straight A's, or being an exemplary Christian! God delights in me no matter what my present state of mind is, and no matter how I mess up! God's delight in me does not fluctuate with my actions or moods. God isn't displeased with me when I make a mistake. He is not disappointed in me or disgusted with me for one second my whole life long. God delights in me! He never thinks, *I'm so sorry I saved her!* Or, *You're not really Christian material.* I may feel that way about myself. *I'm the worst Christian in my church!* However, God never thinks that way about me!

Transforming Grace

When I think about the word *delight*, there are pictures of moments in my children's lives that flash through my mind. I think of my precious daughter, Ellie, when she was about three or four years old. She was swinging at the park while I was pushing her. As I pushed, she was laughing, giggling and kicking her feet. She kept shouting, *"Higher – higher – higher!"* in her sweet, high-pitched voice. That's delight. Another moment that comes to mind is that of my gracious daughter, Emily, when she was five years old. Without my help (just supervision), she made her first batch of chocolate chip cookies. We caught her look of delight and admiration with our camera as she held up her achievement for us. That's delight!

There are so many variations of delight. One summer, my husband, Mark, and I went with our church's high school group to summer camp in California. It was fantastic hanging out with such great teens and dedicated leaders. On the day reserved for Disneyland, Mark and I were invited to join a group of freshmen guys. Because I was having a flare-up of rheumatoid arthritis at the time, I rented a wheelchair. You have not really experienced Disneyland until you have been in a wheelchair pushed by a fourteen-year-old young man. *Whoa! Hold on to your hat!* These teenagers delighted in trying new techniques to scare me: wheelies, careening on two wheels around a corner, or being pushed down the hill and letting me go while I screamed, *I'm going to run into somebody – help!* My ride never quit all day! My delight, however, was very small in comparison to that of my son, Daniel, when we rode on the Tower of Terror. Oh yeah, there's nothing like the Tower of Terror to delight a fourteen-year-old, especially when he looks at his mom whose fingers have turned pale from her death grip on the rail! The more anxious I got, the happier he grew! That's delight: shining eyes, exuberant happiness, shouts of joy and exhilaration!

Does it seem too far-fetched, then, to say that God delights in us? That's precisely what God feels, and that's what He thinks! He's delighted in us; it is His heart towards us. He looks at us with delight, and His eyes are shining. His heart simply overflows with joy. I checked the meaning of the English word *delight* on my computer. According to the online dictionary,[10] it is defined as, *A high degree of pleasure, enjoyment, joy, rapture.* Rapture? This is incredible! It's amazing to think that the Scripture actually says that God is enraptured with us. He enjoys His thoughts of us to the *highest* degree.

---

[10] www.dictionary.com

Transforming Grace

Because I considered that perhaps the Bible word for *delight* might be something a little less exuberant, I looked it up as well. The Hebrew word, *'chaphets,'* which is translated in our English Bible as *delights* means *to incline to, to bend, to be pleased with, to desire, to have or take delight in.*[11] The Hebrew and English words mean the same thing: God delights in you and me. He is always looking at us through eyes of loving grace. God is so delighted in us that He can't stop thinking about us! Look again at the first part of the Hebrew definition of *'chaphets:'* *To incline to, to bend down.* God delights in you so much that He is not just standing

---

[11] Vine's Expository Dictionary of Biblical Words, Copyright © 1985, Thomas Nelson Publishers.

aloof and only taking an occasional glance in your direction. *Oh, how is she doing?* No! He's like a parent with a young child who is right down on the infant's level as he takes his first step. *Come on, come on! Come to Daddy.* Mommy and Daddy have the camera out as they eagerly capture the precious moment. That's God's position! He is inclined. He is bent down. His whole attention is focused on us, because He delights in us so much! God delights in you; He delights in me.

Well, I get it. I understand the idea, but why don't I experience this kind of joy in my life? Why don't I feel God's delight and approval on a daily basis? Why do I feel like I am just sledging through life's never-ending routine of work, responsibilities and stress while under a cloud of disapproval and condemnation? Why does it feel like this if God delights in me? Those are good questions, and to understand the source of our dilemma we need to look at the opposite view of God's attitude towards us.

The opposite of thinking *God delights in me*, is thinking, *God condemns me* or *God is angry with me.* Sometimes, we think this is the way God views us, but it is the opposite of God's thoughts towards us. The cause of our feelings of disapproval and condemnation, however, stems from living under the Law.

Transforming Grace

The Bible declares that the person who believes in Jesus is <u>not</u> under the condemnation of Law! *Therefore there is now no condemnation for those who are in Christ Jesus.*[12] The Bible assures us that we are not saved by what we do or don't do. Salvation is a gift of God's grace, and it isn't earned. God freely lavishes His grace anyone who will accept His Son, Jesus. This is the foundation for how to be <u>saved</u> by grace. However, Christians may struggle with <u>living</u> in grace because the tendency of everyone is to think that God's approval is based on our performance. Living under Law rather than experiencing a life lived in grace is so pervasive! It is in our nature

---

[12] Romans 8:1 (NASU)

to feel condemned for not achieving certain standards.

Let's examine what it means to be under the Law. In the Old Testament, the Law was all the commandments that God gave to the Jewish people. It included the Ten Commandments, but actually was comprised of 613 commandments. Try posting those on your wall and keeping them every day! Do you think you could remember them? Actually, no one succeeded at this and everyone was guilty of breaking at least some of God's 613 commandments. That's why the Apostle Peter later said, *Now therefore why do you put God to the test by placing upon the neck of the disciples **a yoke which*** *neither our fathers nor we have been able to bear?*[13] Nobody could keep the Law!

Fortunately, we are no longer under obligation to obey the Old Covenant laws. For example, we don't have to avoid pork. We don't have to worry about keeping a certain day for worship, hand washing rituals, and all of the various things associated with keeping kosher. Although we no longer deal with the Law in that sense, there are still a lot of us (if not most of us) that live under some kind of law that we have placed on ourselves. Wanting to do what is good and right is not living under the Law. We desire to do what is right because we are saved. We're new

---

[13] Acts 15:10 (NASU)

creations in Christ. What we once loved we now hate, and what we once hated we now love. There is a new person inside of us that loves God and wants to live for God. There is absolutely nothing wrong with that. That's not living under the Law.

What then does it mean to live under Law? Living under Law is characterized by a performance-based life. It's all about what I do and what I don't do. It includes not just my actions, but also what I say and what I don't say. It's not just the bad stuff I do, but also the good stuff that I neglect to do. I can beat myself up with this type of standard, can't I? I know I'm not the only one who has struggled with living under Law!

Many people have the perception that what they do or don't do will somehow make God smile at them a little more. But, our performance has absolutely nothing to do with how God views us. Even on our worst of days, God is delighted with us. On our best of days, He is not more delighted in us. His heart towards us never changes. He is the same *yesterday, today, and forever.*[14] We can never disappoint Him! How could we disappoint Someone who has foreknowledge? He already knows everything about us. After God saved us (and we've sinned even after that moment), God wasn't surprised by anything we did or said. God never exclaimed in surprise, *I can't believe I*

---

[14] Hebrews 13:8 (NLT)

saved her! I didn't <u>know</u> he was going to do such a thing; can we somehow get his name out of the Book of Life? He <u>knows</u> the way we think, and when He has refined us, we will come forth as gold. We're not gold right now. We're like ore that is in the process of being ground and refined, and all the impurities taken out. We're not beautiful yet, but we will be some day.

This is how we feel if we are living under the Law: We feel discouraged and depressed when we fail. When we don't feel like going to church because we've been so selfish and ugly to our spouse, *that's* living under the Law. When we can't look someone in the eye, smile and say, *God loves you and so do I* because we've been so grumpy – *that* is living under the Law.

Some other signs that indicate we may be living under the Law include:

1. Feeling a nagging sense of competition or comparison with other people. If we look to compare ourselves with 'Suzy Christian' who we perceive to be better than we are, then guess what? We will always find a 'Suzy Christian' who is better than we are! Nevertheless, God is delighted in both us **and** Suzy! He loves all of us equally!

2. Feeling judgmental of ourselves or of other people.

3. Feelings of condemnation.

4. Showing and/or feeling disapproval of our own actions or those of others.

5. Feeling as though we are not good enough.

6. Believing that we are a failure.

Any of these thoughts and feelings may be symptoms of living as if we're under the Law.

At this point, we need to address the question, *Is there ever a time when a person* **should** *be 'under the Law'?* There are at least a couple of situations in which it is valid to feel convicted and condemned as under the Law. First of all, if you are not a Christian, you *are* under the condemnation of the Law. Secondly, if you are a Christian but you have chosen to live in a sinful lifestyle, or you have chosen to hang onto sin, then you are under the conviction of the teachings and commands of the Bible.

There is a proper use of the Law and there are good reasons to feel convicted or condemned. If you are not a Christian, God uses the Law. But, how does a secular person know what is right from wrong? We live in a society that values and promotes an independent and self-determined way of life. Many people live as if there are no real absolutes. Only a generation or two ago, most people believed in moral absolutes.

For example, it was commonly believed that marriage was a lifetime commitment between one man and one woman, and that sex outside of marriage was wrong. Today, our families are disintegrating through divorce. We know that the family is being redefined in many ways such as single parent families, parents that aren't married but living together and other variations on the traditional family. Proponents of same-sex marriage are taking their case to the ballot box and the courts. The battle for traditional morality is fierce. We can't look to the culture for moral guidance, so our Creator has given every one of us an inner warning system that sounds an alarm when we do wrong. It's called our conscience. Some people, however, have ignored their conscience to the point that they don't hear its alarm.

God has also given us moral absolutes that are found in the Bible. God's Word declares that there are definitely things that are wrong. It's wrong to murder. It's wrong to steal. It's wrong to cheat. It's wrong to lie. It's wrong to gossip. It's wrong to have sex outside of marriage between one man and one woman. The Scripture tells us that all of these things (and more) are morally wrong. If you're not a Christian and you are feeling bad about doing some of these things, that's good! You should feel guilty. The right purpose of the Law is to point out your moral failures and turn you to God, so that you can confess,

Transforming Grace

God, my life is a mess. I need You. You know what? God delights in forgiving and accepting anyone who will admit their moral failures (sin). He happily sweeps you up in His arms and accepts you as His child.

Jesus said, *"All that the Father gives Me will come to Me, and the one who comes to Me I will certainly not cast out."*[15] If you have never acknowledged that there is a God, and that you have done things that are morally wrong, take this opportunity to turn away from your sinful, self-determined life and turn to God. You can pray a simple prayer in your heart to God. Pray with me and accept this gift of love that God wants to give you. He

---

[15] John 6:37 (NASU)

wants to accept you as His very own child and totally transform your life to give you the hope of eternal life with Him after you die. If this is what you want, let's pray this prayer:

"Dear God, I thank You that You are a God of love and grace. You have rules and standards, and they are good! I have not acknowledged You, and I have been living my life my own way. I have done things that are wrong; my life is not right as far as what You say. Please forgive me for (insert your failure here). I want to be Your child and receive the gift of hope and life forever with You. I ask You to accept me and to look at me with delight as Your child. I accept the gift You are giving to me of being part of Your family and of having all my sins

Transforming Grace

forgiven by what Jesus did in dying on the cross and shedding His blood for me. Thank You. I accept Your gift, and I thank You for accepting me. In Jesus' Name. Amen."

Welcome to God's family! The good news is that you are no longer under the condemnation of the Law! Jesus has forgiven you, and God looks at you with delight. You are not under the Law.

Now, what if you are a Christian and you are still acting and feeling like you are living under guilt and condemnation? You may feel down, discouraged or have a nagging sense of guilt. Is there any reason a Christian will feel the condemnation of the Law? Yes, if you are a Christian and you are choosing to live a sinful lifestyle, you **should** feel guilty. You will notice that I didn't say that you inadvertently slipped into sin. We all do that! If there is something in your life that you know is wrong, and you won't let go of it for some reason, then it is good that the Law says something to you like, *That's not right!* You should understand that it is wrong and you should feel bad about living in that sinful lifestyle. Please understand that I am not talking about slipping and falling. I'm not talking about the sins that we all commit just because we make mistakes. What I am singling out is a resolute attitude expressed as; *I am going to do this! I don't* **want** *to let go of this!* If you are a Christian, and you are hanging onto something sinful in your life, making it your lifestyle, then you should feel guilty for that choice. That's a proper use of Law. You are under the Law in that sense. You aren't lost, but you are being convicted by the Holy Spirit and by God's Word that the lifestyle of sin that you have chosen is not what God wants for your life.

If that describes you, seek out a mature Christian, a pastor (or other Christian leader) or a Christian counselor. Tell them, *Hey! I am caught in this sinful pattern, and I need to confess it.* The Scripture tells us to *confess our faults to one another, and pray for one another that we might be healed.* (James 5:16) Sometimes sin gets a grip on us because it is hidden, and we haven't confessed our sin and become accountable to someone who could help us. We need to tell someone and make ourselves accountable. Give permission to a particular individual to come up to you and ask, *How is it going?* That is code for *How's it going with this sin that has been entangling your life?* This is a good thing, and it will help you to find freedom from a sinful lifestyle or habit. Sometimes you get so tied up that you can't even lift a pinkie finger to help yourself. You need mature Christians around you who can help take off those ropes and set you free from the sin that is binding you. *Confess your faults one to another and pray for one another that you might be healed.*[16]

---

[16] Galatians 6:1 (NASU)

Transforming Grace

Many of us, however, are struggling with living in grace and cannot attribute it to a deliberate determination to hang onto sin. We love the Lord and really want to live in a way that honors the love and grace He has extended to us. Yet, we continue to struggle with condemnation and feelings of failure and spiritual inadequacy.

Christians have been set free from the Law to live a life in the freedom of grace. I'm just as prone as anyone to forget that I'm living in God's great grace and act like I'm under Law. When I was initially preparing the Women's Retreat message that has become the rough draft for this chapter, I was so discouraged because my study time seemed to be sabotaged! Every time I tried to sit down with God's Word and write this chapter, something out of my control went awry. First, my computer was knocked off the network at church, and the technician on staff had to work on it during the entire time I had set aside for study. The very next day, when I had cleared another block of writing/study time, I got an emergency call that filled the rest of my day. I lost my study time again! I was fretting, *Okay, I've got to get this done by the deadline, and now there are no large blocks of time left.* It was a personal nightmare. There was no time in the Word, no time to hear from God as to what He wanted me to write, and the deadline was looming in front of me.

On top of the time crunch, I was worn out because the week before I had been at high school camp. (It was a blast, but I'm not a teenager anymore!) Then, on this particular day, I was so done with rheumatoid arthritis! *I'm done! It's over! I quit! This is it! I'm tired of chronic pain and fatigue and the costly treatments that don't seem to do anything. If one more well-meaning person offers advice on yet another folk remedy, I'm going to say, 'DO NOT TELL ME SOME NATURAL CURE BECAUSE **I'M DONE WITH THAT TOO!'** I'm done with it all! I'm done with the disease and I'm done with the cures!* I didn't want to go to the doctor, and that day I had to go in for my medication treatment that involved an IV for several hours. I didn't want to get poked again. So I stomped into my doctor's office with *attitude.* I complained to the receptionist, *I don't want to sit here for an hour before I get called!* I grumbled to the nurse who actually came within a mere five minutes to take me back for the treatment. I griped at her as she was putting the blood pressure cuff on my arm. While the nurse practitioner was prepping me, examining, poking and checking my joints for range of motion, I griped, complained and moaned at her! *I'm so sick of this treatment! It doesn't work. I've been doing it for two years and it hasn't changed a thing. I can't live this way.* I had fallen into a very dark, self-centered pit. And, in the middle of all of this, these thoughts were running through my mind:

*I'm not being a good witness here! What if she knew I was a Christian? Oh, I hope she doesn't know my husband is a pastor! How can I be such a grouch? And **I'm trying to write a study on living in the joy of grace!** I have nothing to say. I'm the last person God would want to use; I **am such a failure!***

What was fueling my despair? I was under the Law. I was camping in *Law Land*. I had my tent pitched, my generator running, and I was cooking 'stew' in Law Land! In the middle of my tirade, this nurse practitioner looked me in the eye and said, *I'm so proud of you for staying engaged in your health care.* **What?** She continued, *Most people just give up, and you are an amazing woman to keep going with this disease!* I was ready to cry! There was a lump in my throat and my eyes were welling up as I thought, *What a sweet person! She's so encouraging when I'm such a complainer.* It didn't even occur to me that God may have been reaching out to me to show His love and grace.

A few minutes later when I was sitting in the infusion room with a heating pad on my arm, waiting for the nurse to insert the IV, I heard the Lord speak to my heart. All He said was, *I'm bending down right now.* Just five little words, but I knew what He meant: **He's delighted in me**! *You are delighted in me, the* *complaining, griping, Christian pastor's wife who has just blown her witness to a whole office staff?*

God delights in us apart from our performance and attitudes. His delight is a gift of His grace.

The goodness of God leads you to repentance. (Romans 2:4 NKJV) I was able to say, *You know, Lord, I'm sorry! Thank You that You love me no matter what! Nobody else could love me like You do. Your love and grace are so amazing; You delight in me even when I'm a crab!* God **always** delights in us.

Grace is not camping in *Law Land* saying, *I'm so bad! I'm so horrible!* Let God pick you up and carry you through the difficult times in your life. That's living in grace. 1 John 4:16 says, *We have come to know the love which God has for us...* Every Christian knows that God loves him, so the Apostle adds three significant words - *...**and have believed!** We have come to know **and have believed** the love which God has for us.*[17] We know God's love, don't we? We know God's grace, mercy and compassion. We know that He delights in us. Even with this knowledge, however, we must choose to live in His grace. We must <u>believe</u> His love and grace covers all our lives - not just our past failures but also our present and even our future mistakes. Read 1 John 4:16 like you believe it! If you don't believe it, read it until you do!

---

[17] 1 John 4:16 (NASU)

Transforming Grace

> *We have come to know and have believed the love which God has for us.*

You believe it! You do, don't you? *He loves us! He delights in us!* Believe it; hang onto it. Don't let the enemy entice you to camp in 'Law Land.' Stay in grace. I really like how Eugene Peterson paraphrased this verse: *We know it so well, we've embraced it heart and soul, this love that comes from God.*[18]

So, what does it mean to live in grace? That's what we want to experience! We want to experience God sweeping us up

---

[18] *(THE MESSAGE: The Bible in Contemporary Language copyright 2002 by Eugene H. Peterson. All rights reserved.)*

off of our feet, and dancing with us in this beautiful dance of joy. We want to cry out, *Draw me after you and let us run together.*[19] We've been set free through God's grace to live in the joy of freedom from guilt and condemnation and the assurance of God's complete love and acceptance. All the time… every day of our life! He doesn't ever send us on the Guilt Trip; we're on the *Grace Trip* with God.

Let's pray:

Father, we thank You that You delight in us and that You are carrying us in this beautiful, glorious, exhilarating dance of grace. Lord God, if we have been camping in

---

[19] Song of Solomon 1:4 (NASU)

Transforming Grace

Law Land, help us to move out of Law and freely enjoy living in the glow of Your gracious delight. In Jesus' Name, Amen.

Bible References

Chapter Eight